I0843739

# WAYS TO HANDLING EMOTIONS:
# A practical guide to master and manage your emotions and feelings.

Jack Coleman

All rights reserved. No part of this publication may be reproduced, distributed, or transmitted in any form or by any means, including photocopying, recording, or other electronic or mechanical methods, without the prior written permission of the publisher, except in the case of brief quotations embodied in critical reviews and certain other noncommercial uses permitted by copyright law.

Copyright © Jack Coleman,2022.

# Table of contents


Chapter 1

Chapter 2

Chapter 3

Chapter 4

# Chapter 1

**What are Emotions?**

Emotions are reactions that human beings feel in response to events or circumstances. The sort of emotion a person feels is determined by the scenario that causes the feeling. For instance, a person feels delighted when they get excellent news. A person feels fear when they are threatened.

Emotions have a strong influence on our daily lives. We make choices depending on whether we are pleased, angry, sad, bored, or annoyed. We select activities and pastimes depending on the feelings they evoke. Understanding emotions may help us navigate life with better comfort and steadiness.

In their book "Discovering Psychology," authors Don Hockenbury and Sandra E. Hockenbury believe that emotion is a complex psychological state that has three distinct components: a subjective experience, a physiological reaction, and a behavioral or expressive response.In addition to trying to explain what emotions are, researchers have also sought to identify and classify the different varieties of emotions. The descriptions and insights have developed over time.

In 1972, psychologist Paul Ekman argued that six fundamental emotions are universal throughout human cultures: fear, contempt, rage, surprise, happiness, and sadness.In the 1980s, Robert Plutchik invented another emotion classification system known as the "wheel of emotions." This concept demonstrated how diverse emotions may be combined or mixed, much the way an artist combines essential colors to make other colors.In 1999, Ekman broadened his list to include a range of other essential sentiments, including embarrassment, excitement, disdain, humiliation, pride, pleasure, and comedy.

## Key Elements of Emotions

To better appreciate what emotions are, let's focus on their three key parts, known as the subjective experience, the physiological reaction, and the behavioral response.


- Subjective Experience

While experts say that there are a handful of core universal emotions that are experienced by everyone all over the world regardless of background or country, studies also indicate that feeling emotion may be quite subjective.

Consider fury, for example. Is all rage the same? Your own experience might range from modest discomfort to flaming rage. We also don't always perceive pure representations of each sensation. Mixed feelings concerning numerous events or conditions in our lives are prevalent. When presented with commencing a new work, you might feel both happy and apprehensive. Getting married or having a baby might be described by a vast variety of sensations ranging from happiness to fear. These sensations might occur simultaneously, or you can experience them one after another.


● Physiological Response

If you've ever felt your stomach lurch with anxiety or your heart palpate with panic, then you realize that emotions may produce powerful physiological reactions.

The autonomic nervous system directs automatic body functions, such as blood flow and digestion. The sympathetic nervous system is charged with guiding the body's fight-or-flight reactions. When presented with a threat, these reflexes rapidly prepare your body to escape from danger or meet the attacker head-on.

While early studies of the physiology of emotion tended to concentrate on these autonomic reflexes, more recent work has addressed the brain's participation in emotions. Brain scans have indicated that the amygdala, part of the limbic system, plays a significant role in emotion and fear in particular. The amygdala itself is a tiny, almond-shaped area that has been associated with motivational states such as hunger and thirst as well as memory and emotion. Researchers have employed brain imaging to reveal that when people are exposed to threatening imagery, the amygdala becomes involved. Damage to the amygdala has also been found to influence the fear response.

- Behavioral Response

The fourth component is perhaps one that you are most familiar with—the actual expression of emotion. We spend a considerable amount of time analyzing the emotional signals of the folks around us. Our ability to successfully interpret these expressions is tied to what psychologists term emotional intelligence, and these expressions have a crucial impact on our total body language. Sociocultural norms also have an impact on how we express and experience emotions. In Japan, for example, people seek to repress displays of fear or scorn when an authority figure is near. Persons in the United States are more prone to express negative sentiments both alone and in the presence of others, but persons in Japan are more likely to do so when alone.

## Types of Emotions

There are many theories as to how many forms of emotions humans experience. As noted, psychologist Paul Ekman identified the following six universal emotions:

Happiness: Many people seek happiness because it is a pleasant sensation accompanied by a sense of well-being and enjoyment. Happiness is generally indicated by smiling or speaking in an upbeat tone of voice.

Sadness: All of us feel sadness now and then. Someone might display sadness by weeping, being quiet, and/or withdrawing from others. Types of sadness include grief, despair, and disappointment.

Fear: Fear may boost heart rate, generate racing thoughts, or promote the fight-or-flight reaction. It could be a reaction to true or imagined hazards. Some folks appreciate the adrenaline rush that accompanies fear in the form of watching terrifying movies, riding roller coasters, or skydiving.

Disgust: Disgust may be aroused by a physical experience, such as seeing or smelling rotting food, blood, or insufficient hygiene. Moral disgust may emerge when someone watches another person doing something they find immoral or disgusting.

Anger: Anger may be exhibited by facial expressions like frowning, yelling, or violent action. Anger may motivate you to make changes in your life, but you need to find a healthy outlet to express anger so it doesn't cause harm to yourself or others.

Surprise: Surprise may be pleasurable or unpleasant. You might open your lips or gasp when you're shocked. Surprise, like fear, may provoke the fight-or-flight response.

# Chapter 2

## What affects your emotions

Emotional Intelligence is an integral aspect of a full individual. It is the capacity to detect and regulate your own emotions and the sentiments of others. Emotions drive people, people drive performance. These sentiments might be considered as the power source, which brings about performance in individuals. For a person to be able to generate an amazing result, his or her emotions have a vital function to play in how they operate and acquire outcomes.

A person going through sadness or stress will create little or no output. Emotions, which may also be characterized as human energy, bring about productivity and thus translates to high or poor performance.

Exercise: Notice if you are in a good mood when you get to a decision point. Or shut your eyes and recall anything that makes you generally happy: a favorite television program, studying, conversing with a buddy, resting for a few minutes with a book, or having a nice chuckle. Remembering anything emotionally nice can bring up that wonderful mood.

When it comes to the job, numerous emotions affect productivity:

Short-lived Emotions: These forms of emotions are impacted by what is occurring at a certain moment. Most times, these sensations are generated by several stimuli of the moment. Examples are Anger, Fear, Disgust, Excitement, etc.

Long-term Emotions: This has to do with a person's mood fluctuation, which may either be negative or good. This might lead to a person fully shutting down or being in a cheerful state of mind. Example: Depression.

Personality Traits or Dispersion: This includes a certain attitude, which a person might acquire according to his or her surroundings. For example, growing up in a home with so much hatred and anger might alter how a person perceives life.

Most people are uninformed of the energy that pours from them. Emotions are so strong that a human emits these sensations intentionally or involuntarily. Others are ignorant of the cause, triggers, and the power these emotions have on their life - how it affects them, the people in their space, and eventually, how to regulate it.
In the world today, several difficulties might impact a person's state of mind, such as traffic, marriage, money, economics, etc. These disorders might create stress on the body. The idea of stress has to do with how a person sees his presence in an environment. Stress slows a person down and generates chemicals such as Cortisol, which might limit his or her productivity. Research

throughout the years has revealed that 85 percent of success or productivity in life is dependent upon how emotionally intelligent a person is, and the first degree of emotional intelligence comprises Self-Awareness.

Each emotion, for example: pleased, sad, worried, optimistic, and more, may be ideally matched to increase your performance in particular sorts of jobs. Although we may not always be conscious of it, much of the jobs we do, whether we are replying to a colleague's email or participating in a difficult negotiation with a supplier have a lot to do with our emotions. The reason emotions have a surprisingly profound influence on our performance is that they have adaptive value, which helps individuals manage and react to the circumstances at hand.Good emotional health begins with being aware of your thoughts, emotions, and actions. Learning healthy strategies to deal with stress and issues is a natural part of life. Feeling comfortable about yourself and having healthy connections are vital.Many things that happen in your life might affect your emotional wellness. These may lead to severe emotions of melancholy, stress, or worry. Even desirable or desired changes may be as stressful as unwanted ones. These items include:

A pandemic
Being laid off from your work.
Having a kid depart or return home.
Dealing with the loss of a loved one.
Getting divorced or wedded.
Suffering a disease or an injury.
Getting a job promotion.
Experiencing money troubles.
Moving to a new house.
Having or adopting a baby.

Your body reacts to the way you think, feel, and behave. This is one sort of "mind/body connection." When you are worried, nervous, or disturbed, your body responds physiologically. For example, you could acquire high blood pressure or a stomach ulcer following a highly stressful incident, such as the loss of a loved one.

Path to Improved Health: There are techniques to enhance your emotional health. First, notice your feelings and understand why you are experiencing them. Sorting out the sources of depression, stress, and worry in your life might help you manage your emotional health. Following are some more useful recommendations.Express your emotions in suitable ways.If emotions of stress, grief, or worry are creating health difficulties, holding these sentiments within might make you feel worse. It's good to let your loved ones know when something is troubling you. However, bear in mind that your family and friends may not always be able to help you cope with your emotions effectively. In these instances, seek someone outside the issue for aid. Try contacting your family doctor, a counselor, or a religious adviser for guidance and assistance to help you improve your mental health.

Live a balanced existence.Focus on the things that you are thankful for in your life. Try not to worry over the difficulties at work, school, or home that contribute to unpleasant sentiments. This doesn't imply you have to pretend to be joyful when you feel worried, nervous, or sad. It's vital to cope with bad sentiments but try to concentrate on the good things in your life, too. You may wish to use a diary to keep notes of things that make you feel joyful or serene. Some study has indicated that adopting a positive mindset may enhance your quality of life and give your health a boost. You may also need to discover strategies to let go of certain things in your life that make you feel worried and overwhelmed. Make time for activities you like.

Develop resilience.

People with resilience are better at healthily dealing with stress. Resilience may be developed and improved in several ways. These include having social support, retaining a good opinion of oneself, embracing change, and keeping things in perspective. A counselor or therapist may assist you to attain this aim via cognitive behavioral therapy(CBT). Ask your doctor whether this is a good idea for you.

Calm your mind and body.

Relaxation activities, such as meditation, listening to music, listening to guided imagery tapes, yoga, and Tai Chi are excellent strategies to bring your emotions into balance. Free guided imagery films are also accessible on YouTube.

Meditation is a sort of directed thinking. It may take numerous forms. For example, you may accomplish so by exercising, stretching, or breathing deeply. Ask your family doctor for guidance regarding relaxing strategies.

Take care of yourself.
To have excellent mental health, it's necessary to take care of your body by establishing a regular schedule. This involves a schedule of good food, sleep, and exercise to alleviate pent-up stress. Avoid overeating and don't overuse drugs or alcohol. Using drugs or alcohol merely produces additional concerns, such as family and health problems.

Things to Consider;
Poor mental health might impair your body's immune system. This makes you more susceptible to catching colds and other diseases during emotionally challenging periods. Also, when you are feeling pressured, apprehensive, or disturbed, you may not take care of your health as well as you should. You may not feel like exercising, eating healthful meals, or taking medication that your doctor recommends.You may misuse alcohol, cigarettes, or other

substances. Other indications of low emotional health include:

back pain
change in appetite
chest pain
constipation or diarrhea
dry mouth
extreme weariness
general aches and pains
headaches
high blood pressure
insomnia (trouble sleeping)
lightheadedness
palpitations(the feeling that your heart is racing)
sexual troubles
lack of breath
stiff neck
sweating
upset stomach
weight gain or decrease

## How Your Emotions Influence Your Decisions

According to Herbert Simon, American Nobel Laureate scientist, "To have anything like a full account of human reason, we have to understand what function emotion plays in it."

As Dr. Simon and others have pointed out, emotions impact, distort or even entirely dictate the result of a significant number of choices we are presented with within a day. Therefore, it behooves those of us who want to make the best, most objective judgments to know everything we can about emotions and their influence on our decision-making. But, just in case you're not convinced about what I and Dr. Simon said, and you continue to think you can make judgments devoid of emotional bias, let's look at how emotions are produced and how they are translated into actionable sentiments.

First, every sensation starts with external input, whether it's something someone said or a physical experience. That input triggers an unfelt emotion in the brain, which drives the body to manufacture response hormones. These hormones enter the circulation and cause sensations, sometimes unpleasant and sometimes favorable. So, to recap, it's stimuli, then emotions, then hormones, and, last, sensations. In other words, your emotions affect your decision-making process by producing specific sentiments.

According to another specialist in the area, American-Portuguese neuroscientist Dr. Antonio R. Damasio, the brain continually has to refresh its knowledge about the body's status to govern the myriad processes that keep it alive. And, it needs to transform those emotions into actionable feelings. In an ever-changing environment, this is the only way a creature can live. For instance, when we feel threatened by anything, the first sensation is called "fear." That fear, employing hormones, results in the formation of fight-or-flight responding emotions, enabling our body to react rapidly and correctly for its self-preservation. This emotional response comes swiftly and involuntarily. Then, generally after an exceedingly short amount of time, we become aware of those changes. We become aware of them only when response hormones have reached our system and we experience them as a sensation of being terrified or possibly inferior. Awareness that there is a continual and intricate dance of emotions and moods might considerably increase your emotional intelligence, including your decision-making capacity. However, to assist in your comprehension of the topic, let me introduce you to Paul Ekman's Emotion Wheel.

To continue with our fear to frightened/inferior example above, we can look at the Emotion Wheel to more clearly picture that "fear" on the inner circle is distinct from "frightened" on the outer one. Or, to redirect our emphasis to the positive, we may utilize the Emotion Wheel to observe that the emotion of "happy" in the inner circle might result in a sensation of "joyful," "powerful" or even "proud" in the outer circle.

All well and good you might say, but how does knowledge of this help us make decisions that are genuinely advantageous in the long term, and not, perhaps, only regarded as beneficial in the short run? We achieve it by concentrating on the subsequent sensation. In other words, we need to analyze how any given emotion (the inner circle) will convert into a sensation (outer circle) (outer circle).The benefit is in knowing that the six emotions are merely broad categories with little precision, whereas the experiences are more comparable to how we genuinely and precisely express what's going on in our minds and bodies. For example, we can observe that the feeling of disgust is essentially a universal repulsion. Without the Emotion Wheel, it's hard to discern how it converts into details, i.e., emotions. Only when we observe this ultimate consequence can we successfully apply knowledge of emotions and sentiments in the decision-making process. Instead, if we strive to comprehend that any certain emotion, say, disgust, will result in a sense of, say, "loathing" "judgmental" or "detestable," then we may better analyze the situation and choose the appropriate action. To practice, let's choose an issue you wish to deal with and make a choice. Except, this time we will accomplish it from the particular to the general, rather than from the general (the inner circle) to the specific (other circles) (other circles). After you have recognized and picked an item from the outside circle, trace that sensation inside via the two rings until you have reached the fundamental emotion (the inner circle) (the inner circle).

Using this approach, you may observe that although you believe you are experiencing a sensation, you are dealing with an emotion. Sometimes, I think of our sensations as symptoms of our emotions. So, as in dealing with most ailments, you need to go to the main cause (an emotion) rather than a symptom (a sensation) (a feeling).

So, how can you build a functioning understanding of this process, to improve decision-making? Here are some items I find useful:

• Name what you are deciding. You don't need the Emotion Wheel for this, but you do need to analyze precisely what the issue is and the repercussions of your suggested remedy.

• Recognize and identify whatever emotions you are experiencing concerning the choice. These sensations will very sure occur someplace on the outer circle of the Emotion Wheel.

• Bring your sensations inside via the middle circle to uncover its fundamental cause (an emotion) (an emotion).
• Process that emotion, not one of its symptoms (a sensation) (a feeling).
• Be conscious of whether you want to choose from this precise feeling or whether you want to modify the route.

Of course, you also need to do all the normal things you commonly hear about as favorable to objective decision-making, such as avoiding making choices while you are sleepy, worried, or being affected by non-objective actors. Nevertheless, addressing the fundamental or emotional foundation of your sentiments will go a long way toward enhancing your decision-making.

# Chapter 3

**How to regulate your emotion**

The capacity to feel and express emotions is more vital than you may imagine.As the emotional response to a specific event, emotions play a significant influence on your responses. When you're in touch with them, you have access to critical information that assists with:

decision-making

relationship success

day-to-day interactions

self-care

While emotions may play a positive function in your everyday life, they can take a toll on your mental health and interpersonal relationships when they start to seem out of control.A therapist says that any feeling even exhilaration, delight, or others you'd generally see as good may escalate to a point where it becomes impossible to regulate.With a little work, however, you can take back the controls.

Two research from 2010 demonstrates that having high emotional control abilities is associated with well-being. Plus, the second one discovered a probable correlation between these talents and financial success, so putting in some effort on that front may pay off.

Here are some tips to get you started.

1. Take a look at the influence of your emotions

Intense emotions aren't all negative. "Emotions make our life intriguing, distinctive, and vibrant,""Strong sensations might suggest that we accept life wholeheartedly, that we're not denying our natural reactions."It's entirely natural to suffer some emotional overflow on occasion— when something fantastic occurs when something tragic happens when you feel like you've missed out. So, how do you tell when there's a problem?

Emotions that routinely go out of control could lead to:

connection or friendship conflict

difficulty connecting to others
trouble at work or school
an inclination to use drugs
physical or emotional outbursts.

Find some time to take stock of precisely how your uncontrolled emotions are influencing your day-to-day existence. This will make it easy to identify problem areas (measure your progress) (and track your success).

2. Aim for regulation, not repression
You can't manage your emotions with a dial (if it were that simple!). But suppose, for a minute, if you could regulate emotions this way.You wouldn't want to keep them running at maximum all the time. You also wouldn't want to shut them off totally, though.When you suppress or repress emotions, you're blocking yourself from experiencing and expressing them. This might happen intentionally (suppression) or subconsciously (repression).Either may lead

to mental and physical health issues, including:
anxiety
depression
sleep difficulties
muscular strain and pain
difficulty managing stress
substance usage

When learning to exert control over emotions, be sure you aren't merely brushing them under the rug. Healthy emotional expression entails striking some balance between overpowering feelings and no emotions at all.

3. Identify what you're experiencing
Taking a minute to check in with yourself about your emotions will help you begin getting back in control.Say you've been seeing someone for a few months. You tried booking a date last week, but they indicated they didn't have time. Yesterday, you texted

again, adding, "I'd want to meet you soon. Can you meet this week?"

They eventually react, more than a day later: "Can't. Busy."

You're suddenly terribly agitated. Without pausing to think, you fling your phone across the room, knock over your wastebasket, and kick your desk, stubbing your toe.Interrupt yourself by asking:

What am I experiencing right now? (disappointed, perplexed, furious) What occurred to make me feel this way? (They blew me off with no explanation.)

Does the circumstance have an alternate explanation that would make sense? (Maybe they're worried, unwell, or coping with something else they don't feel comfortable sharing. They could aim to explain more when they can.)

What do I want to do about these feelings? (Scream, release my rage by tossing stuff, send back something unpleasant.)

Is there a better method of dealing with them? (Ask whether everything's OK. Ask when they're free next. Go for a stroll or run.)By examining different alternatives, you're reframing your thinking, which might help you adjust your original extreme response.It might take some time before this reaction becomes a habit. With experience, going through these processes in your thoughts will become simpler (and more successful) (and more effective).

4. Accept your feelings, all of them.
If you're attempting to grow better at controlling emotions, you can try downplaying your sentiments to yourself.
When you hyperventilate after hearing wonderful news or fall on the floor screaming and weeping when you can't locate your keys, it can seem beneficial to tell yourself, "Just calm down," or "It's not that big of an issue, so don't panic out."
But this invalidates your experience. It is a significant thing to you.Accepting emotions as they arrive helps you grow more comfortable with them. Increasing your

comfort with overwhelming emotions helps you to completely experience them without responding in severe, unproductive ways. To learn to accept emotions, consider thinking of them as messages. They're neither "good" nor "bad." They're neutral. Maybe they bring up terrible emotions occasionally, but they're still sending you essential information that you can utilize.

For example, try:

"I'm frustrated because I keep forgetting my keys, which makes me late. I should put a dish on the shelf near the entrance so I remember to leave them in the same place."

Accepting emotions may lead to increased life happiness and fewer mental health issues. What're more, individuals thinking of their emotions as beneficial may lead to greater levels of enjoyment.


5. Keep a mood diary

Writing down (or typing out) your emotions and the reactions they cause might help you discover any disruptive tendencies.

Sometimes, it's enough to mentally trace feelings back via your thoughts. Putting sentiments into paper might help you to ponder on them more profoundly.It also helps you realize when particular conditions, like problems at work or family strife, lead to harder-to-control emotions. Identifying particular triggers makes it possible to come up with solutions to handle them more successfully. Journaling delivers the greatest value when you do it every day. Keep your diary with you and write down powerful emotions or sensations as they happen. Try to notice the triggers and your response. If your reply didn't assist, utilize your notebook to explore more beneficial alternatives for the future.

6. Take a deep breath
There's plenty to be said about the power of a deep breath, whether you're wildly joyful or so upset you can't speak.Slowing down and paying attention to your breath won't make the feelings go away (and remember,

that's not the purpose).Still, deep breathing exercises may help you center yourself and take a step back from the initial acute flash of emotion and any excessive response you wish to avoid.

The next time you sense emotions beginning to take control:Breathe in gently. Deep breaths originate from the diaphragm, not the chest. It may help to envision your breath rising from deep in your abdomen.Hold it. Hold your breath until a count of three, then let it out slowly.

Consider a mantra. Some individuals find it beneficial to repeat a mantra, such as "I am calm" or "I am relaxed."

7. Know when to express yourself

There's a time and place for everything, even deep emotions. Sobbing uncontrollably is a relatively frequent reaction to losing a loved one, for example. Screaming into your pillow, even hitting it, could help you express some rage and anxiety after being rejected. Other instances, though, call for some moderation. No matter how furious you are, yelling at your supervisor over an unjust disciplinary action won't help. Being attentive to your surroundings and the circumstance might help you understand when it's OK to let emotions out and when you might want to sit with them for the time being.

8. Give yourself some space

Getting some space from overwhelming sensations might help you make sure you're responding to them in sensible ways.This distance could be physical, like leaving a distressing environment, for example. But you may also establish some mental space by diverting yourself. While you don't want to ignore or avoid emotions totally, it's not bad to divert yourself until you're in a better situation to deal with them. Just make sure you do come back to them. Healthy distractions are only brief.

Try:

taking a walk

watching a hilarious video
talking to a loved one
spending a few minutes with your pet

## 9. Try meditation

If you practice meditation already, it could be one of your go-to ways for dealing with overwhelming emotions.Meditation may help you expand your awareness of all emotions and events. When you meditate, you're training yourself to sit with those emotions, to observe them without criticizing yourself or seeking to alter them or make them go away. As noted, learning to embrace all of your feelings may make emotional management simpler. Meditation helps you strengthen those accepting abilities. It also has additional advantages, including helping you relax and enjoy better sleep.

## 10. Stay on top of stress

When you're under a lot of stress, controlling your emotions might become more challenging. Even persons who typically can regulate their emotions effectively could find it tougher in times of intense tension and stress.Reducing stress, or finding more effective methods to handle it, might help your emotions become more bearable.

Mindfulness activities like meditation may assist with stress, too. They won't get rid of it, but they can make it simpler to live with.

Other good strategies to deal with stress include:

getting adequate sleep

making time to converse (and laugh) with friends

exercise

spending time in nature

making time for leisure and hobbies

## 11. Talk to a therapist

If your emotions continue to seem overpowering, it may be time to seek professional assistance.Long-term or chronic emotional dysregulation and mood fluctuations are connected to various mental health problems, including borderline personality disorder and bipolar disorder. Trouble managing emotions might also connect to trauma, familial troubles, or other underlying challenges.

A therapist may give sympathetic, judgment-free assistance as you:
identify variables leading to dysregulated emotions
address severe mood swings
learn how to down-regulate intense feelings or up-regulate limited emotional expression
practice challenging and reframing feelings that cause distress.

Mood swings and intense emotions can provoke negative or unwanted thoughts that eventually trigger feelings of hopelessness or despair.This loop might ultimately lead to maladaptive coping mechanisms like self-harm or even thoughts of death. If you begin thinking about suicide or have cravings for self-harm, speak to a trusted loved one who can help you receive assistance right immediately.

# Chapter 4

## Improving Emotional Intelligence (EQ)

When it comes to pleasure and success in life, EQ counts just as much as IQ. Learn how you may enhance your emotional intelligence, develop better relationships, and accomplish your objectives.

What is emotional intelligence or EQ?
Emotional intelligence (sometimes known as emotional quotient or EQ) is the capacity to understand, utilize, and control your own emotions in constructive ways to reduce stress, communicate successfully, empathize with others, overcome problems, and diffuse conflict. Emotional intelligence helps you develop better connections, thrive at school and work, and accomplish your professional and personal objectives. It may also enable you to connect with your emotions, put intention into action, and make educated choices about what matters most to you.

Emotional intelligence is generally described by four attributes:

Self-management — You're able to regulate impulsive sentiments and actions, manage your emotions in healthy ways, take initiative, follow through on promises, and adjust to changing situations.

Self-awareness — You realize your own emotions and how they affect your thoughts and conduct. You recognize your skills and flaws and have self-confidence.

Social awareness - You have empathy. You can comprehend the feelings, wants, and worries of other people, pick up on emotional clues, feel comfortable socially, and grasp the power dynamics in a group or organization.

Relationship management - You know how to build and maintain excellent relationships, communicate effectively, inspire and influence people, work well in a team, and handle conflict.

Why is emotional intelligence so important? As we know, it's not the brightest individuals that are the most successful or the most pleased in life. You undoubtedly know folks who are intellectually smart and yet are socially incompetent and unsuccessful at work or in their relationships. Intellectual capacity or your intelligence quotient (IQ) isn't enough on its own to accomplish success in life. Yes, your IQ may help you get into college, but it's your EQ that will help you handle the stress and emotions while confronting your final examinations. IQ and EQ exist in combination and are most successful when they build off one another. Emotional intelligence affects your performance in school or work. High emotional intelligence may help you manage the social difficulties of the workplace, lead and encourage people, and flourish in your profession. When it comes to judging critical job prospects, many firms now regard emotional intelligence as vital as technical skill and implement EQ testing before hiring.

Your physical health. If you're unable to regulate your emotions, you are probably not managing your stress either. This may lead to major health complications. Uncontrolled stress elevates blood pressure, inhibits the immune system, increases the risk of heart attacks and strokes, leads to infertility, and speeds up the aging process. The first step to enhancing emotional intelligence is to learn how to handle stress.

Your mental health. Uncontrolled emotions and stress may also damage your mental health, rendering you subject to anxiety and despair. If you are unable to comprehend, become comfortable with, or regulate your emotions, you'll also fail to create solid connections. This in turn might leave you feeling lonely and alone and further worsen any mental health issues.

Your connections. By knowing your emotions and how to regulate them, you're better equipped to convey how you feel and comprehend what others are experiencing. This helps you to communicate more effectively and establish deeper connections, both in business and in your personal life.

Your social intelligence. Being in touch with your emotions has a social function, connecting you to other people and the environment around you. Social intelligence helps you to discern friends from the adversary, gauge another person's interest in you, relieve stress, regulate your nervous system via social contact, and feel loved and joyful.

## Building emotional intelligence

Four critical skills to enhancing your EQ
The abilities that make up emotional intelligence may be taught at any moment. However, it's crucial to understand that there is a difference between merely

studying EQ and implementing that information into your life. Just because you know you should do something doesn't guarantee you will, especially when you feel overwhelmed by stress, which may overrule your best intentions. To permanently modify behavior in ways that hold up under strain, you need to understand how to overcome stress in the present, and in your relationships, to stay emotionally aware.

The primary abilities for strengthening your EQ and boosting your capacity to handle emotions and interact with people are:
Self-management
Self-awareness
Social awareness
Relationship management

Key skill 1: Self-management
For you to engage your EQ, you must be able to use your emotions to make constructive decisions about your behavior. When you become overly stressed, you can lose control

of your emotions and the ability to act thoughtfully and appropriately.

Think about a time when stress has overwhelmed you. Was it simple to think clearly or make a sensible decision? Probably not. When you get extremely stressed, your ability to both think clearly and appropriately analyze emotions—your own and other people's—becomes hampered. Emotions are crucial bits of information that tell you about yourself and others, but in the face of stress that puts us out of our comfort zone, we might get overwhelmed and lose control of ourselves. With the capacity to regulate stress and be emotionally present, you may learn to accept painful information without letting it overpower your ideas and self-control. You'll be able to make choices that help you to control impulsive impulses and actions, regulate your emotions in healthy ways, take initiative, follow through on promises, and adjust to changing situations.

Key skill 2: Self-awareness
Managing stress is simply the first step to growing emotional intelligence. The science of attachment reveals that your present emotional state is likely a mirror of your early life experience. Your capacity to handle key emotions such as anger, sorrow, fear, and joy generally relies on the quality and regularity of your early childhood emotional experiences. If your main carer as a newborn understood and respected your emotions, your emotions have probably become significant assets in adult life. But, if your emotional experiences as a baby were unclear, scary, or traumatic, you've probably sought to detach yourself from your feelings. But being able to connect to your emotions—having a moment-to-moment connection with your shifting emotional experience—is the key to understanding how emotion impacts your ideas and behaviors.

Do you experience sensations that flow, meeting one emotion after another as your experiences vary from moment to moment?

Are your emotions accompanied by physical sensations that you feel in regions like your stomach, neck, or chest?

Do you experience individual sentiments and emotions, such as rage, sorrow, fear, and pleasure, each of which is reflected in subtle facial expressions?

Can you have overwhelming sensations that are strong enough to captivate both your attention and those of others?

Do you pay attention to your emotions? Do they play into your decision-making?

If any of these sensations are unusual, you may have "turned down" or "turned off" your emotions. To increase EQ—and become emotionally healthy—you must reconnect to your fundamental emotions, embrace them, and feel comfortable with them. You may attain this via the practice of mindfulness.

Mindfulness is the discipline of purposefully concentrating your attention on the present moment—and without judgment. The practice of awareness has origins in

Buddhism, although most faiths contain some form of comparable prayer or meditation approach. Mindfulness helps change your obsession with cognition toward an appreciation of the present, and your bodily and emotional feelings, and gives a greater perspective on life. Mindfulness calms and concentrates you, making you more self-aware in the process.

Key skill 3: Social awareness
Social awareness helps you to detect and analyze the mostly nonverbal clues people are continually employing to communicate with you. These clues allow you to realize how people are feeling, how their emotional state is changing from moment to moment, and what's genuinely important to them. When groups of individuals give out comparable nonverbal signs, you're able to read and grasp the power dynamics and shared emotional experiences of the group. In short, you're sympathetic and socially comfortable.

Mindfulness is an ally of emotional and social awareness.

To create social awareness, you need to acknowledge the role of mindfulness in the social process. After all, you can't pick up on small nonverbal signs while you're in your thoughts, thinking about other things, or just zoning out on your phone. Social awareness needs your presence in the present. While many of us pride ourselves on our ability to multitask, this implies that you'll miss the subtle emotional changes going on in other people that let you fully comprehend them. You are more likely to advance your social objectives by laying other ideas aside and concentrating on the conversation itself. Following the flow of another person's emotional reactions is a give-and-take process that demands you to also pay attention to the changes in your own emotional experience. Paying attention to others doesn't weaken your self-awareness. By spending the time and effort to properly pay attention to people, you'll acquire insight into your emotional condition as well as your values and beliefs. For example, if you experience uncomfortable hearing people voice particular opinions, you'll have learned something significant about yourself.

Key skill 4: Relationship management
Working successfully with others is a process that starts with emotional awareness and your capacity to perceive and comprehend what other people are feeling. Once emotional awareness is in play, you may successfully build additional social/emotional abilities that will make your interactions more effective, profitable, and gratifying. Become aware of how well you utilize nonverbal communication. It's tough to avoid delivering nonverbal cues to others about what you think and feel. The various muscles in the face, particularly those around the eyes, nose, lips, and forehead, assist you in wordlessly transmitting your feelings as well as

interpreting other peoples' emotional intent. The emotional component of your brain is constantly on and even if you disregard its signals others won't. Recognizing the nonverbal cues that you convey to others may play a major role in enhancing your relationships.Use comedy and play to ease stress. Humor, laughter, and play are natural antidotes to stress. They lighten your responsibilities and help you keep things in perspective. Laughter puts your nervous system into balance, lowering tension, calming you down, sharpens your thinking, and making you more empathetic. Learn to perceive disagreement as a chance to develop closer with people. Conflict and disputes are inherent in human interactions. Two individuals can't reasonably have the same wants, views, and expectations at all times. However, it needn't be a terrible thing. Resolving disagreements in healthy, productive ways helps improve trust between individuals. When disagreement isn't regarded as dangerous or punitive, it

supports freedom, creativity, and safety in
partnerships.

www.ingramcontent.com/pod-product-compliance
Lightning Source LLC
Chambersburg PA
CBHW071114260726
48661CB00006B/2612